BeLoved:
14 Days on Love, Loneliness, Relationships, & Redemption

By Jordan Lee

Formatted and edited by Katie Erickson

ISBN-13: 978-1540666970
ISBN-10: 1540666972

Table of Contents

Hey girlfriend!

I'm so stoked you've chosen to do this study!

You know, regardless of our romantic relationship status, I think we all wrestle with love, loss, and relationships and all that good stuff. For that reason, God put it on my heart to write a study on the subject of relationships without it being exclusively about romantic relationships or directed toward any specific relationship status demographic.

If you're single, this study is for you. If you're casually or seriously dating, this study is for you. If you're engaged or hoping to be married someday, this study is for you. If you're married, this study is for you. If you're widowed or divorced, this study is also for you. Love and redemption go so far beyond a relationship status, although that is what our world often fixates on.

It's a matter of the heart, because it's an integral part of who we are. This whole thing is so much more about hearts than it is about our status. I think it's about time we start paying attention to that.

So yeah, you are welcome here. If you're lonely or tired or weary or broken or thriving right now, you're welcome here. I pray that my silly little quips and stories fill your heart with joy while God's Word fills your heart with the true, real, life-changing love and truth that we all so desperately need.

Anyway, thank you for your willingness and openness to letting God lead you to this study.

You seriously totally rock.

Be loved, beloved.

xox,

jordan lee

For more, follow me online!
Facebook: **Jordan Lee**
Instagram: **@soulscripts**
www.thesoulscripts.com

day 1: baggage isn't sexy

2 Corinthians 3:17
Galatians 5:1, 13-14
Romans 8:14-15

A few weeks ago, I had to fly across the country for work. When I left for the airport, I felt pretty good about myself. I had somehow figured out how to throw together a sweet little outfit (fashionistas may have scoffed at it, but I liked it, so whatever) and even managed to curl my hair and throw on a splash of my favorite Marc Jacob's Daisy perfume.

I parked my car in long term parking and made the trek towards the terminal. At first, I felt great. But as I lugged my purse, work briefcase, and suitcase in the hot sun, my armpits started sweating and sweat beads formed on my forehead.

GREAT.

When I finally arrived inside the terminal and stood in line to check my bags, I felt a lot less cute than I did when I parked my car. To make matters worse, I somehow dropped my purse and spilled all the contents onto the floor. I scurried to clean it all up and gracefully held up the line in the process.

Cue more sweating from my embarrassment

I finally got my bag checked but then the flight was delayed… and delayed… and delayed again… and again. After hours of waiting and lugging around my carry-on bags from gate to gate, the flight was canceled.

For the record, I was not feeling cute in any way at this point. I was actually pretty ticked. Then, after all of that, I had to stand in line for two hours just to retrieve the suitcase I had checked so that I could stay in a hotel for the night.

I was salty and I felt like a hot mess as I lugged my bags BACK to my car that just happened parked a million miles away.

sad violin playing

As I drove away in the rain, I began to think about how much trouble my baggage caused me on a day like that. It made me slower, sweatier, and stinky-er.

The baggage wore me out and dragged me down. I can't help but think that that's exactly what the baggage we carry in our hearts does to us, too. I believe it slows us down. It wears us out. It hurts our confidence in God, relationships, and ourselves, and it can really stink, too.

When I first started dating Matt, we both carried some baggage into the relationship. I struggled with a hard heart after a rough breakup, and he struggled with trust after being burned by past relationships. But it's something we found freedom from with a little bit of honesty and grace.

I don't know what kind of burdens your heart is lugging around. Maybe it's sexual shame or past hurt that's harming your ability to step out of the terminal and into the airplane. Perhaps it's something else. But I do know that you have free checked bags when you trust in Christ Jesus.

When He died on that cross, He took your shame, your hurt, your pride, and all the other baggage you're carrying into your relationships. Shame tries to define who you are, not what you've done or what's been done to you.

The Savior has given you unlimited access to freedom.

So, check your bags. Drop your brokenness at the cross today, and fly the friendly skies in freedom.

GET IT OUT

Write down everything that's weighing you down. What's holding you back? What fears or past hurts or anxieties affect your ability to step forward?

_____

_____

_____

_____

_____

_____

_____

_____

_____

_____

_____

TRUTH SAYS...

2 Corinthians 3:17 says that where the Spirit of the Lord is, there is freedom from whatever is holding you back

Galatians 5:1 mentions the yoke of slavery. Anything can enslave us, especially fear, regret, doubt, trust issues, and past hurts. But Christ has set you free. You are not a slave to the past or past relationships.

Galatians 5:13-14 is a powerful reminder that you were called, made, and destined to be free, and that freedom should be used for God's glory – to serve, to sacrifice, and to love others well. It's hard to love someone if your arms are tied in bondage. Let Him untie them so you can take steps toward faith

THE BIG IDEA: I AM NOT A SLAVE TO THE PAST

PS. Writing this truth in big letters across the top of the pages of Galatians 5 in my Bible helps etch the big idea into my brain! Try it!

Day 2: single as a pringle (not just for single girls)

Isaiah 54:5
Jeremiah 31:3
Mark 3:33-35
1 Corinthians 7:7

As a kid, I *loved* Pringles. My poor parents would have to hide the Pringle can from me or I'd eat them all in one sitting.

Now, I want you to think about a Pringle. It's shaped in such a way that it's made to be stacked. It's designed so that it can be squished up nice and tight next to a bunch of other Pringles and fit in the can properly, right? Right. Okay, great. Moving on.

I think we're a lot like Pringles. I don't mean that we're salty (although sometimes that's true, too). I mean that Pringles are designed for stacking – for community, relationship, connection with other Pringles so that they fit where they belong (in the Pringle can).

In the same way, we are designed for community, relationship, and connection with other people. We have an innate need to feel that we belong. But when one Pringle gets taken off the stack, it is no longer just a part of the Pringle community. I think this is why singleness can feel so painfully lonely at times. I ALSO think that this is why we can feel painfully lonely even within relationships. Isolation from connection and relationship is terrifying because we are designed to be stacked, fitted close next to another. Our hands fit together just like Pringles fit together. It's simply the way we're made.

So, when we feel that we have no one to our right or left, it's scary and it's lonely, and we don't have to be "single" to feel this way. Many married women feel isolated and alone because true community is more than just a status – it's a connection. It's not uncommon for that connection to be lacking.

One can feel single without actually being single.

Anyway, here's my point: I know sometimes feeling alone is scary – it's uncertain what will happen next. Will we get eaten alive? Will we die alone?

But before we begin to worry, we have to remember that each Pringle was paid for and loved. Think about it. A snacker, or a consumer or Pringles, values each individual Pringle. Each one may have a few different ridges or chipped edges from other Pringles, but that doesn't make it any less valuable.

Singleness is not better or worse than marriage – both are a gift. Don't downplay singleness because the world tells you to get busy making a family. You have a family, a kingdom family.

So, if you're feeling lonely, or if your edges are chipped and your ridges are rough, remember that you are highly valued by the One who bought you at a high price. You are designed for community, even if you aren't experiencing romantic companionship.

If you don't feel like you have a place to belong in the Pringle can (the dating community), you always have a place to belong in the factory (God's community).

Despite your shortcomings, lost love, loneliness, or cracked edges, He will claim you as His and make you a part of His Kingdom – stacked high full of Pringles.

GET IT OUT

In what ways have you felt alone, isolated, or inadequate? What triggers those feelings?

_____

_____

_____

_____

_____

_____

_____

_____

_____

_____

_____

TRUTH SAYS...

Isaiah 54:5 says that your Maker is your husband. You were made for Him and He gives Himself to you in your very breath.

Jeremiah 31:3 says that you are loved with an everlasting love. Everlasting means unending, unchanging. Your feelings of isolation do not determine how loved and valued you really are.

Mark 3:33-35 is the words of Jesus claiming the profound truth that YOU are part of His family. Again, you're not ever as isolated as you feel.

STUDY TIP

Draw connections between these verses, highlight them, and write these truths in the margin next to them (feel free to use the note taking methods from my book *Brighten Your Bible Study*). These Scriptures are all from different books of the Bible, but if we look closely, we'll see how carefully they are woven together with a grace-filled strand.

THE BIG IDEA: MY RELATIONSHIP STATUS DOES NOT DETERMINE MY WORTH

Day 3: distance makes the heart grow

Isaiah 40:28-31
Hebrews 12:13
Philippians 3:13-14
2 Timothy 4:7-8
Deuteronomy 31:6

In college, I started running long distance as a way to escape the stress of school. After several months of running 7, 8, 9, and even 10 miles almost daily, I decided to sign up for a local half marathon.

When I woke up on race day, I looked out my window to see that it was a cold, rainy October day. Motivation level? Zero.

Somehow I convinced myself to follow through and showed up at the designated location, only to find out that it was a trail race through the hilly terrain. Unfortunately, I hadn't read the fine print when I signed up during Economics class (oops). I had never trained for a trail run, and again I strongly considered backing out. Luckily, a good friend was with me and she urged me on, encouraging me that I could do it.

Several times throughout the race I wanted to stop. The path in front of me was so long and I wished God would make the hills a little flatter and the air a little warmer. But when I thought about quitting, I stopped looking out and looked up.

Each and every time I did, a little glimmer of sunlight shone through the trees and revived my heart enough to keep me going. Despite the several times I wanted to give up, I completed the distance and made it to the end. I even had enough energy to sprint through the finish line!

It was one of the most difficult physical challenges I've faced in my life, but I felt like a champion when I crossed that finish line.

Similarly, throughout our whole engagement, Matt and I lived long distance. At times, we would get discouraged and feel that we were growing more distant than we were closer together.

When we'd become really frustrated, we would feel distant from God AND each other. To be honest, there were moments that I wanted to give up. Why? Because the human heart longs for closeness – with its Maker and its match. When it feels distant, it grows weary.

And when it grows weary, it wants to give up.

If you're feeling distant, please know that it's normal and not hopeless. Whether you're facing separation from someone you love and feeling like giving up, sensing distance from your spouse in your own home, or even feeling distant from God, take this as your reminder to endure and finish the race.

I know it's hard. I know it's a long, hilly road with twigs and rocks in the way that are just dying to trip you up.

You may even be weary or anxious about all the "what if"s:
What if it's really hard? What if it hurts? What if God doesn't answer my prayer?

But when the "what-ifs" start running your heart, keep running forward and respond with: *"So what?"*
So what if it's hard? So what if it hurts? So what if God doesn't answer my prayer? **SO WHAT?**

When the distance stretches your heart, even when it hurts, remember that you are a champion in the making.

You CAN run this race even when it hurts, even when God doesn't do what you want God to do (like make the hills flatter), and even when you grow weary.

When you begin to doubt that, look up. I promise, you'll see a little glimmer of hope shine through the trees.

GET IT OUT

Write down any feelings of distance that are making you weary. Is there someone you are missing? Is your heart aching and tired? Do you feel distant from God? What can you do to lessen the distance?

_____

_____

_____

_____

_____

_____

_____

_____

_____

_____

_____

TRUTH SAYS...

Isaiah 40:21-28 reminds us that when we grow weary in our faith, hope, or relationships, God is everlasting. He does not get tired. He will strengthen us when we have no strength left.

Hebrews 12:13 says that although the road may be long and hard, we can run the race set before us because the Spirit gives us power to endure.

Philippians 3:13-14 and 2 Timothy 4:7-8 encourage us to keep our eyes on the prize (Jesus) and to press on in our present troubles toward eternal glory.

Deuteronomy 31:6 is a profound promise to hold onto when we feel distant from God and those we love. He promises that He is not far away; He is not distant even when we are. We can be strong and courageous in pressing on because we never have to do it alone.

CHALLENGE:

Take a moment to stop and pay attention to God. We experience more of what we pay attention to. If we pay attention to the long path in front of us or to the weary feeling in our legs and hearts, then we will experience more discouragement and weariness. But when we look up through the trees and pay attention to the God of hope, strength, and endurance, we will experience more hope, strength, and endurance.

THE BIG IDEA: ENDURE TO THE END

Day 4: when you want to fix him

Proverbs 15:1, 19:13
1 Peter 3:16
Matthew 7:3

When I was a little girl, I helped my daddy build a swing set for our backyard. It was a really nice wooden one, with two swings AND two slides. That was fancy-shmancy back then and I couldn't help but get in on the action.

We pounded nails into the boards and built up the frame. We worked tirelessly until it was exactly how we wanted it. Well, I ate an orange popsicle and wore my Little Mermaid swimsuit, but hey, I cheered dad on as he worked.

Flash forward. There was a point in my relationship with Matt where all the big differences between us seemed to expose themselves all at once.

We realized I was a planner and he was a procrastinator. We realized that I was loud and vocal in arguments, while he was quiet and pensive (which drove me crazy for a while). I hated driving around for hours but it was his favorite thing to do on a Sunday afternoon. I'm an organized neat freak but he's more relaxed about messes. The list goes on.

When our differences frustrated me for the first time, I just wanted to fix it – to put everything back to the way it was before, when it was easy and I could just stand there and not work at it, maybe even enjoying an orange popsicle.

Ah yes, just the way I like it.

But in the middle of these newfound differences, I realized that there will be certain behaviors and differences I don't necessarily understand or like in my spouse. But I can't just move the boards of his heart, and pound nails into his head when he's not acting or functioning how I would prefer. Force divides rather than unifies and the hammer certainly never works – not in a fruitful way, anyway.

Whether you've been married for many years, dating, or simply hoping to meet your match, it's important to remember that people are broken with flaws and they're going to let you down sometimes.

He won't meet your every need and he won't do everything right. You can't fix his flaws with a hammer and nails and you can't change his ways. But God can.

The best tool you have is prayer. I urge you to use it regardless of your relationship status. In doing so, remember that the Lord has the whole workshop.

Entrust your frustrations to the Master Craftsman and He'll sand down those sharp edges, one ridge at a time.

GET IT OUT

Consider the things that frustrate you about someone you care about. How have you approached those things? In what ways have you (or have you not) been inviting God into those areas? Write them down.

_____

_____

_____

_____

_____

_____

_____

_____

_____

_____

TRUTH SAYS...

Proverbs 15:1 reminds us to choose gentleness over anger, yes, even if it is the millionth time. You have the power to powerfully choose one or the other.

Proverbs 19:13 illustrates the damage of quarreling. Before allowing anger to boil over again, before trying to fix or change the current struggle, step back and ask: does this specific concern hold eternal weight? If not, quarreling is nonproductive and damaging.

1 Peter 3:16 reminds us that Christ-like behavior can win over the heart of another. This doesn't mean that it's okay for us to get walked all over, and there are instances where professional help or separation is needed. However, this truth encourages us to submit to the throne of grace when dealing with a difficult spouse. When we bow at His feet and stand in awe of the grace we've been given, we are empowered and equipped to give grace and act in a Christ-like way.

Matthew 7:3 reminds us to look in the mirror. It can be hard to hear, especially when we've been hurt, but what is the speck a part of? The log. These words of Jesus remind us of this hard reality: the faults that anger us the most about others are often the ones that we despise most within ourselves.

CHALLENGE:

If you're considering dating a man who doesn't support or understand your faith, realize you can't change him permanently. He may make some behavior changes, but true change is a transformation of the heart. If your guy has some frustrating flaws, consider if they are character flaws or just annoyances. If you're married and living with a difficult spouse, remember the power that prayer has over the hammer. If you're not married, be intentional about seeking a partner who isn't perfect but is purposeful in His pursuit of the Lord.

THE BIG IDEA: SHUT UP AND PRAY

Day 5: not today, satan!

John 15:9-10
1 John 4:9-11, 18
Ephesians 6:10-14
Romans 5:8
Proverbs 3:15

Have you ever had a salesman come to your door and try to sell you a product you don't need? Or have you ever been walking through a mall and have one of those people at a booth come up to you as you're sprinting to the food court (oh, that's just me? Sorry, I love food.) to hand you some hand cream or eye cream or anything else to fix your flaws? If you haven't experienced that, perhaps you've had cold calls with a stranger on the other end of the line offering you the next best deal.

Unfortunately, I've experienced all three of those things and every single time I just want to scream, *"NOT TODAY, SATAN!"*

I always somehow restrain the urge to yell, "GO AWAY!" and instead respond with a polite little, "Oh, not today, thank you though."

But you know what? I believe a lot of women struggle with feeling worthy of love. I can't tell you how many emails I've received from girls who worry the man they love will change his mind and walk away, or how many women feel insecure in their relationships and wonder if they're a good enough wife or girlfriend.

I also know this because I've experienced these ugly feelings as well. I've worried one day Matt will wake up and realize all the crazy he's marrying into. I've worried that I'm not a good enough of a cook, encourager, housekeeper, friend, human, etc. for him. I've even worried if I'm worthy of God's love with all my crazy broken parts that tend to get all out of whack when I haven't had my coffee or time with Jesus.

But if we look a little closer, we will see those thoughts for what they really are: door to door sales. Cold calls. Poor quality eye creams from mall booths. Sales pitches from the devil asking me to open the door of my heart and let him in.

Sometimes, I make the mistake and let him come in and sit on the couch of my heart. Sometimes, I answer the phone and listen to the pitch from the man on the other end, and buy it. Sometimes, I take the packet from the guy at the mall and smother it on my face even if it doesn't work. Maybe you have, too.

But when the enemy begins to sell you the idea that you're not worthy of love, not good enough and in need of some cream to mask your flaws, you don't have to be polite.

You have permission to raise your voice and say: NO, SATAN. YOU WILL NOT COME IN HERE AND TRY TO STEAL MY IDENTITY. I AM A DAUGHTER OF GOD NOT A GIRL IN DISTRESS. I AM REDEEMED, MADE NEW, COMPLETE, AND WHOLE IN CHRIST. YOU ARE NO LONGER WELCOME HERE WITH YOUR LIES.

Then slam the door.

If what you're listening to doesn't line up with Truth, then it's a lie.

Truth says, "Yes, you're broken and yes, you're a sinner. But you are loved so much that your brokenness is redeemable."

There's no room for inadequacy or evil thoughts to take root in a heart resting in promise like that.

GET IT OUT

What voices are you listening to? Are you feeling inadequate, comparing yourself to other women or other relationships? What is feeding and fueling the lies you're believing? Write down every source, every experience, and everything that fuels those feelings.

_____

_____

_____

_____

_____

_____

_____

_____

_____

_____

TRUTH SAYS...

Read the power verses listed for today and you'll find that regardless of who you think you are, regardless of how unlovable you believe you are or how lonely you feel, Abba God has something much different—much better—to say about you.

THE BIG IDEA: I AM SO WORTH LOVING.

Day 6: about that purity thing

1 Corinthians 10:1214
Psalm 51:10
Ephesians 5:714
Romans 3:23

I don't wash my car often, but when I do, I'm sure to clear off every stitch of dirt.

When I'm finished, the old girl is super shiny and I feel like a rock star driving around town. It looks good, right? It looks clean and perfect, from the outside.

What my fellow motorists don't see is the inside of my car. More than likely, it needs to be vacuumed and there's probably an old Starbucks cup (or five) rolling around the floor.

I'm sharing this little insight into my old little car because I think it paints a strong picture of the way we look at the idea of purity. I think it's something we need to be more real and honest about, because everybody struggles with purity, regardless of his or her physical activity.

This may be TMI, but I struggled with masturbation for several years as a teenager. By the time I realize it was a sin, it had already become an ugly habit.

On the outside, I kept a shiny, clean reputation but on the inside I felt so dirty and stuck, until I finally began to talk about it. At the time, it was really hard, but God allowed me to walk through that struggle and find freedom from it so that I can give the hope message to others who may be secretly struggling with their own form of sexual sin – masturbation, infidelity, sex outside of marriage, pornography, whatever it is.

I'm not ashamed to talk about that time in my life, because I think sexual sin and struggle has far too many women in bondage. But the reality is that there's no way to find freedom from it without opening up the doors of our hearts, exposing it to the light, and talking about it.

If your confidence rests in Christ, the judgmental glares you may get have no hold on your heart. And you have the power to do that.

Wherever you are on the purity scale, please realize that you're not hopeless and that grace hasn't run out for you when you think it has. Although I don't know the specifics of your struggle, I do know that you are a daughter and that you're no worse or better than His other daughters.

When you open the doors of the car, when you look into the heart of the matter, there's dust and impurities in all of us. There is more than sexual purity.

There is such thing as emotional purity, too. Are we guarding our hearts and protecting our minds? It's not just about what so-and-so did with that guy.

So, this can't be a comparison thing, nor can it be a self-righteous thing. God doesn't like promiscuity, but He also doesn't like pride. Both of these separate our hearts from His true, good, and real love.

But the good news is that all things are redeemable. This has to be a full dependence and reliance kind of thing, because we can't rely on our own car washing abilities to purify us from the inside out.

Why? Because eventually we'll drive through a mud puddle and what really matters is the inside, the heart of the matter. In other words, we can't be pure on our own.

Worry less about another girl's shine and more about letting Him strengthen you by vacuuming out the shame and struggle that are cluttering your heart.

Open the door, invite Him in, and let Him work from the inside out.

GET IT OUT

Be really honest with yourself and God. What sexual struggle, frustrations, or shame are you facing? Do you feel stuck? What are you afraid of?

_____

_____

_____

_____

_____

_____

_____

_____

_____

_____

_____

_____

TRUTH SAYS...

1 Corinthians 10:12-14 is packed with two powerful truths for when something gets really, really, really, really, really (did I say really?) hard. The first is that you're not alone; others have faced what you're facing. It's not weird or abnormal. You're also not forever doomed. God knows your temptation and He will always give you a way out and the strength to overcome it.

Psalm 51:10 reminds us that we cannot create our own pure heart. It's an action of God that He will do when we cry out for help.

Ephesians 5:7-14 tells us that crying out for help also requires vulnerability and humility. If we don't trust the Lord enough to expose our sin and brokenness, then we don't trust Him enough to free us. Shame has a way of shackling our hearts and enslaving us to hiding our sin. But truth tells us that true freedom is found in vulnerability and exposing our weakness, because then our confidence can rest in Christ and not the glares we get from people. The devil has no hold on us then.

Romans 3:23 serves as a powerful reminder not to compare our level of purity to a sister's, because all have sinned and fallen short of the glory of God. We can only look to Jesus.

THE BIG IDEA: VULNERABILITY = FREEDOM

Day 7: rest & trust the best

1 Corinthians 7
Psalm 37:4
Matthew 6:33

One day in the sixth grade I was swinging on the playground and the boy I crushed hard on sat just two swings over from me. I prayed that he would notice me, maybe even like me back, even just for one week.

One week, God, that's not too much to ask, is it?

At the time, it made perfect sense. I just wanted to be noticed and admired, even if only for a moment. It seemed like the best thing in the world. Looking back, it seems like the silliest thing in the world. Why would I want to be noticed only to be forgotten after seven days? **DUMB.**

When that boy finally noticed me, it was exciting. But it hurt my little sixth grade heart when I realized he also noticed several other girls on the playground.

You know, I think it's something women still fall into, at any age. The temptation to settle for momentary attention, even if it's meaningless, is so strong in a culture saturated with love songs and sex and cutesy wedding Pinterest boards creeping and crawling everywhere.

If you're seeking attention, affection, or affirmation (or just longing to not be the single girl anymore), remember that if you are settling for the boy, that's not God's best. But also realize that God's best doesn't necessarily mean a great, godly man. It may very well be the gift of singleness – which is also a gift, okay? Or if you're already married, it may be the gift of commitment or perseverance when it gets hard.

Regardless of what God's best is for each one of us, the truth is we have access to God's best by giving God our attention. Perhaps we just need to shift our attention from making God's best out to mean that he will give us a great guy to what it really means: His very best. Whatever He gives.

When you're walking with the Lord, your desires will begin to look more like His desires for your life. Perhaps that won't include romance, or perhaps it will.

But until you are so okay with that reality that either option is equally as precious to you, your swing won't fly and you'll be miserable.

Sometimes His best isn't quite what we expect, but we are planted right where we are so that we can receive His best for our life – not for the life of our friends or the Internet. All you can see is this moment on the playground, perhaps on the swing, but He sees the whole thing. He sees the boy (p.s. adults can still be boys) you're pining away after, He sees your heart, and He sees your ability to thrive right where you are – single, lonely, crushing, taken, married, or widowed.

So, instead of flying into another's arms, keep swinging and let the Spirit be the wind beneath your wings.

That IS God's very best.

GET IT OUT

What have you been seeking attention, affection, or affirmation from? Has it been from God or something else? Or perhaps, God *and* something else?

_____

_____

_____

_____

_____

_____

_____

_____

_____

_____

_____

_____

TRUTH SAYS...

1 Corinthians 7 reminds us of the benefits and gifts of both marriage and singleness. When we are tempted to settle or to walk away from something hard, it's important to remember that God has placed us right where we are because it's the very best thing for us today. Even the hard things are for our greater good.

Psalm 37:4 says that when we delight in the Lord (and not the fading things of earth), He will give us the desires of our heart. This doesn't mean that He will just give us whatever we want, though. As we walk with the Lord, our desires will look more and more like His desires for our life and we will desire that His will be done through us, in us, and around us. He knows the best thing for us. The more we walk with Him, we will long for that more and more, even when we can't quite understand it.

Matthew 6:33 is a promise that highlights the truth declared in Psalm 37:4. God knows our hearts' needs and desires. When we seek His kingdom, He will not fail to meet the needs of our hearts. If we truly believe this truth, we will no longer need to settle for temporary satisfaction because He promises that all these things shall be added unto us. He will give us His best and meet our every need.

THE BIG IDEA: GOD'S BEST TRUMPS MY BEST

Day 8: the relationship rollercoaster

Isaiah 26:3
Isaiah 41:10
1 John 4:18

If you've ever ridden a roller coaster, you know the feeling you get in your stomach as the cart drops over the edge into a free fall at a million miles per hour. It's exhilarating and freaky and terrifying all at once. It may even cause a little nausea.

When I was a teenager, I loved the thrill of roller coasters. I didn't mind the feeling in my stomach and I didn't fear falling out of the dinky little car that probably hadn't been maintained in several years, simply because I put my full trust in the ride's safety belts.

As I grew older, I noticed myself becoming less trusting of the ride's safety belts. I don't choose to ride coasters so much, and if I do, I hold on much tighter than I did as a kid. I think stepping into new territory – whether that's a new relationship with another human or beginning a relationship with God – can give us that same uneasy, exhilarating, perhaps slightly terrifying feeling. Although it's thrilling, our human nature beckons us to hold on tight with our own strength. It's hard to trust the Safety Belt; it's hard to trust the Spirit. It's especially hard when it feels like our entire life is free falling toward the ground at the speed of light.

When I first met Matt, I knew within just a few days that I would marry him. It was a scary and exhilarating feeling all at once, so much so that I refused to tell my family about him for months because I was afraid I'd mess something up!

If you've been holding on tight in an effort to control the journey, if you've been struggling to trust Him regarding your relationship, open your hands and ask the Lord for peace and clarity. Maybe the "he" in your life isn't trustworthy but **He** is. Maybe the "he" is trustworthy but you've not given that trust as a result of a fear stuck deep in your heart.

All relationships ride a roller coaster, and there will always be ups and downs. But the downs will seem much less severe if you're able to place your trust in the Safety Belt, the Source, the Son, and the Spirit, who sustains and guides all things.

Remember that relationships suffer when there is a lack of trust. When you don't trust God, it becomes incredibly difficult to trust people. So,

take this as a free ticket to loosen your grip, trust
the Spirit, and enjoy the ride.

GET IT OUT

What kind of rollercoaster are you currently riding? Are you experiencing steeps ups and downs in your relationships, or maybe facing uncertainty? Where is your trust lacking? Write down these experiences and feelings.

_____

_____

_____

_____

_____

_____

_____

_____

_____

_____

_____

TRUTH SAYS...

Isaiah 26:3 declares the truth that He will keep peace in those who trust in Him. When we're feeling uneasy and our stomach turns in knots, we have the invitation to be childlike and enjoy the freedom that comes with trusting God through the ride of life.

Isaiah 41:10 and Psalm 56:3 remind us that we have nothing to fear. We can let go of every piece of earthly security we are holding on so tightly to and instead cling to His presence, even when the ride we're on flips us upside down.

1 John 4:8 proclaims the reality that it is impossible to not fear if you do not have love because perfect love drives out fear. God is perfect love, and when you let Him sit next to you through the ups and downs and twists and turns, your fear will subside because of the love you will experience.

THE BIG IDEA: DO NOT FEAR

Day 9: when your heart hurts

Proverbs 3:5-6
Psalm 147:3
1 Peter 2:24
2 Corinthians 5:6-7

I have a friend with a disability that inhibited his ability to walk properly for years. As a boy, he was always slower than the other kids on the playground. He struggled with pain in his joints and was never able to play sports like the other kids.

When he turned 22, doctors suggested a restructuring surgery. Do you know what a restructuring surgery is? It's exactly what it sounds like – a complete rebuilding of his legs. Now, how can one rebuild someone's legs?

Well, you've got to break them first. OUCH!

During the procedure, his fibula and tibia were broken in several places and then the doctors rebuilt them properly, holding them together with countless screws.

The procedure itself lasted several hours and it was almost a year before he could walk again. The poor guy was bed-ridden month after month, heavily medicated to numb the pain. But after the recovery period, his pain subsided and he walked again. Except this time, his legs were healed and he could walk straighter, taller, faster, and stronger than he ever could have dreamed before the restructuring.

You know, sometimes I think we need restructuring, too.

Maybe something has knocked you on your back, and in the midst of the pain you may doubt you'll ever walk again. Perhaps you're in a relationship that drags you down, discourages you, or hinders your walk with the Lord. Or maybe a relationship recently ended or you may have lost a friend. Or maybe, just maybe, that thing you really hoped for failed or disappointed you.

Although I don't know the specifics of your heartbreak, I do know that even though it may really hurt in this season, this isn't how it ends.

Sometimes our hearts need to be broken and rebuilt. So maybe, just maybe, heartbreak isn't really heartbreak at all. Rather, it might just be heart-help.

The periods of recovery and pain allow for healing and rebuilding.

If you're heartbroken, I want to remind you not to numb the pain with quick fixes, but instead let His healing hand work. It might be a slow process, but I promise if you hang in there, you'll be able to walk straighter, taller, faster, and stronger, right into the plans God has for you.

GET IT OUT

What has left you feeling broken hearted? It may be a lost love, loss of a loved one, or a broken friendship. But it could also be feelings of failure, disappointment, or hopelessness. Our hearts can break over much more than lost romance, and your feelings are valid and normal and you're allowed to just sit in them for a moment. Pour out all your yucky on this page, okay?

Let God know where you're at, right now. You're allowed to be broken.

_____

_____

_____

_____

_____

_____

_____

_____

TRUTH SAYS...

Proverbs 3:5-6 urges us not to lean on our own understanding through these seasons. It's hard to understand what is going on and why pain is happening to us in the middle of it. But He understands and He will make us walk again. If we trust Him, we will walk straighter, faster, stronger, and taller.

Psalm 147:3 tells us that like any good doctor, the Lord heals us and binds up our wounds. Sometimes we need a total restructuring of our hearts to know Him better, and the breaking part hurts, but the rebuilding is beautiful. He promises in His Word to rebuild and restore your tiny, beating heart.

1 Peter 2:24 reminds us that Jesus bore the weight of pain, too. God is not too mighty or too distant or too big to understand the pain we experience. This ought to serve as a comfort when we are tempted to think God is not concerned with our problems and pain, even the little things.

2 Corinthians 5:6-7 encourages us to walk by faith and not by sight. It can be daunting to stand up and to step out for the first time after we've been knocked out and paralyzed by pain for a long time. It would be easy to look down, see how weak our legs are, and not even try. But if

we choose to have faith in His work in us, we can walk by faith and not by sight.

THE BIG IDEA: HEARTBREAK CAN LEAD TO RESTORATION, REDEMPTION, AND REVIVAL

Day 10: if you're worried about your love life

Matthew 6:25-27
1 Peter 5:7
Philippians 4:6-7
Philippians 4:19

The other day I sat on a rocking chair, sipped sweet tea, and listened to the birds sing. I know, I sound like I'm 90 years old, but it was nice, okay? As I sat there and rocked back and forth, back and forth, an old phrase came to mind.

It goes something like this: "Worrying is like a rocking chair. It gives you something to do but it doesn't get you anywhere." (Glenn Turner)

Isn't that the truth? Worrying is probably the most nonproductive, paralyzing thing we can do. While it may be comfortable to stay put in the middle of it, listen to the birds chirp, and escape the hurricane that surrounds us, it's a trap and we can't stay there all day.

After a rough breakup in college, I had an awfully depressing month. I felt so lonely that I didn't feel like leaving my house just to see everyone else walking around and holding hands. I watched a lot of TV and ate a lot of chips. I was worried about feeling even lonelier out in society. I was worried about feeling even more out of place than I already did. But my couch was comfortable. It was like the rocking chair I mentioned.

It was nice, comfy, and safe, but also dark and lifeless.

If you're sitting in that rocking chair, worried about problems within your relationship, worried about your lack of relationship, or worried whether or not you'll ever find the right person, take a closer listen to those birds.

Do you want to know why they're singing? The Lord has provided their every need. They've got sunshine, food, breath, and life.

Guess what? So do you.

If He takes care of every need of the sparrow, rest assured, He knows your every need, too, including the need for love – good, strong, healthy, passionate love.

I dare you to stand up from the rocking chair, step a big step of faith off that font porch into His light, and let His love fill that hole in your heart you've been so worried about filling.

And sing ,because you've got nothing to worry about. You just need to believe that.

GET IT OUT

Examine your heart. Have you faced hardships or feelings of isolation from your relationships? Are you worrying that those feelings or problems won't be solved? Are you feeling lonely and worried that God doesn't know your desire for companionship? Are you worried that you'll always be alone? Write down every concern on your heart.

_____

_____

_____

_____

_____

_____

_____

_____

_____

TRUTH SAYS...

Matthew 6:25-27 gives us freedom from these anxieties. If God cares even for the birds' every need, then consider how much *more* He cares for our needs! He has not abandoned your need for harmony or love. He has already provided all the love we need. But our culture is saturated in romance and that makes this truth incredibly difficult to remember. Let this truth etch itself into your heart and hold tightly to it.

1 Peter 5:7 reminds us that when those worries do creep into our minds, we don't have to let them stay there. We don't have to just sit tied to the rocking chair, because we are invited to cast them off us and onto the Lord because He cares for us.

Philippians 4:6-7 again urges us not to be anxious about our lives, but it also offers an invitation to pray and present our worries to God. When we accept that invitation, He will give us a peace that we couldn't concoct on our own with any amount of earthly romance, companionship, or momentary satisfaction. This peace is an eternal peace.

Philippians 4:19 repeats the theme we've seen over and over in this study: God will meet every need of our hearts by the power of His love.

THE BIG IDEA: THE ROCK > THE ROCKING CHAIR

Day 11: Miss independent

John 15:5
Romans 12:4-5

A few weeks ago, I began to put all sorts of pressure on myself to be more, do more, and accomplish more.

Matt had to remind me that we're a team and I don't have to do it alone. He will help me succeed and comfort me when I fail. I couldn't help but think of how much God promises us that same thing.

In the last several decades, there's been a shift in our culture regarding women, and so much of it is good. I'm all about rights, empowerment, and strength for women of all ages.

Independence and empowerment can have pros and cons, however, just like anything else. TOO MUCH independence can cause a person to be incredibly prideful. Now, I'm not saying anyone should ever be dependent upon another person for happiness, worth, etc. Nor am I saying anyone should ever be walked all over. But there is a part of our human makeup that requires dependence.

Let me explain. Before I was born, it would have been absolutely impossible for me to bring two cells together and create my own unique genetic code, right? When I was 10, it would have been ridiculous to think I could independently drive myself to soccer practice. That would just be asking for destruction. And although I'm much more self-sufficient now as an adult, it would be absolutely crazy to think I can generate oxygen for the air I breathe, keep the ecosystem and tilt of the earth on perfect balance, or even tell my heart to beat each second of the day. I'm still relying on something, right?

Although independence, strength, and self-sufficiency are good to an extent, and while we should never suck the life out of another person or expect them to meet our needs in a way only God can, to think we never need help is fooling ourselves and fueling our pride. It's shutting God out of the picture.

Maybe you're afraid of commitment because you're afraid to "lose your independence." Or perhaps you never ask for help from your man because you don't want to be one of those "clingy" or "needy" girls.

Maybe you've stopped praying because a part of you thinks you can handle it on your own. But we need to remember that no matter how empowered or how equal our legal rights are, the reality is that we can't handle it all on our own.

We can't sustain our own life, we can't be machines, and being completely independent is impossible anyway. You really can't "lose" it because it was never something you had full access to anyway. Don't let your pride get in the way of a good guy or a good God.

So, if you're tempted to be Miss Independent, let me just remind you that even celebrities and powerful women aren't that empowered or independent. On earth, they have a whole crew that sustains and supports their work and art. In heaven, they have a God who sustains and supports their very breath.

And so do you.

You are strong only because He is strong. You live only because He lives.

GET IT OUT

What kind of pressure have you put on yourself to be independent? In what ways have you failed to ask God for help? Have you been proud in your relationships or toward God? Write down all the ways you've struggled in this area.

_____

_____

_____

_____

_____

_____

_____

_____

_____

_____

TRUTH SAYS...

John 15:5 is God's reminder that we must not be too proud to depend on Him. Just like a branch cannot produce anything without the vine, we cannot do anything apart from Him. When we believe the lie that we are independent of help, we are foolish, acting like a twig lying on the ground, expecting an apple to grow without being attached to the Source.

Romans 12:4-5 reminds us of our need for others. Every part of the body is important to the overall functioning, and it is foolish for us to think that we do not need the other parts. We are challenged to unite ourselves with others and rely on their functions and not just our own for the sake of the body's proper function. You can let someone in and it won't take away from your own strength or purpose.

THE BIG IDEA:
1. RELY ON GOD
2. ASK FOR HELP
3. THRIVE

Day 12: real dating

John 10:27
Ephesians 2:19
Revelation 3:20

Someone recently told me that it seems so easy for everyone else to experience love, acceptance, and happiness, but that she's had a really hard time figuring out the whole dating thing. She expressed that she can hardly get past the first date. I also recently had a married gal tell me that she's been discouraged because they don't date. Life is busy, the flame has burned out, and the situation is stale.

You see, the reality is that whether we can't get past the first date or have gotten way past the first date, dating can be hard. Life is busy, people are weird, and we worry so much about if it's "right" or "good enough."

Unfortunately, I think the way we date can tend to be a really accurate picture of how we spend time with the Lord. In the beginning, it may be exciting and maybe even a little terrifying. Perhaps we chicken out or doubt ourselves along the way.

If we've been dating awhile and life gets busy, it's also easy to become passive.

But what happens when we put our own preconceived ideas and standards on dating without allowing our hearts to be open? Well, we rarely get past the first date. Or the conversation at dinner stinks. Or the movie night just doesn't happen. Eventually, dating is no longer a priority in our hearts.

Are we allowing Him to lead, guide, move, and stop us dead in our tracks with a dozen roses? Or are we too busy to notice Him?

Growing in a relationship requires noticing and paying attention to the other. If I never praised Matt's performance and efforts in making my day a little sweeter, you can bet we'd have problems. The same goes for God. He's a wild, adventurous, passionate God in pursuit of your heart. Notice. Pay attention. Make dating a priority with both him and Him.

Don't put God in a box because you've been raised to think a relationship with God is a boring, religious requirement. It's an adventure. It's like dating without boundaries or borders. Open your heart, girlfriend. Let His Word be your guide and dive into the adventure.

Your relationship with God (or with a man) shouldn't look like anyone else's.

That's boring and not His way – He's way cooler and more real than that.

GET IT OUT

Write down all the things that have been holding you back from making meeting with God a priority. What are your expectations, and in what ways have those been met or not met? What can you cut back on to make room?

_____

_____

_____

_____

_____

_____

_____

_____

_____

_____

TRUTH SAYS…

John 10:27 talks about knowing God just by His voice. Just like we can't really know or love someone that well without making getting to know them a priority, we can't really know or love God without making getting to know Him and His Word a priority.

Ephesians 2:19 reminds us that God is not too big or too far away for us to develop an intimate relationship with Him. We are part of the party, in the in crowd, invited to dinner, everything. We can be friends with the Lord.

Revelation 3:20 shares the truth that God is constantly at the front door of our heart, just waiting to be let in. Are we too busy to notice?

CHALLENGE:

Before you ask why it looks so easy for everyone else, look inside your heart and ask why it's so hard for you. Are you walking into relationships with men or with God with a closed heart? Do you have strict expectations or rules for how you can get to know them? Is it by your terms only?

THE BIG IDEA: GOD'S PURSUIT OF ME IS HIS PRIORITY. IS MY PURSUIT OF HIM MY PRIORITY?

Day 13: bumper cars

2 Timothy 2:23-24
James 1:19-20
1 Corinthians 13:4-5
John 16:33
James 4:6-10

I love carnivals, but I hate bumper cars. You know, the little ride that requires you to sit in a stinky little cart with rubber bumpers and ram into other stinky cars with rubber bumpers? Yeah, that ride. I never understood the purpose of it.

Oh yes, I'll just sit here and voluntarily get whiplash. Sounds lovely…

After trying the bumper cars thing as a kid, I walked away with a terrible headache and I never wanted to do it again. It honestly beats me why it still exists, but regardless, it does, and people still choose to ride them. I just don't get it.

Regardless of the draw to bumper cars, I think that when we don't see eye-to-eye with the people we love, the result can look a lot like bumper cars – crashes and whiplash and headaches are inevitable if we stay on that ride.

But the difference between bumper cars and us is that we can be reconciled through gospel grace. While Scripture is clear that the Lord wants us to be equally yoked in spousal relationships, the reality is that many people give their life to Christ long after saying "I do."

I'm not here to tell you whether or not your relationship is a good one or not based on your individual faith – that's a personal discernment between you and God. But if you have deep seated doubt about it, that's likely not a coincidence. However, another reality is that bumps and crashes can still happen between two people who love the Lord. People are people, and people are different, and people are broken and make mistakes.

If you're feeling like you're in the middle of the bumper zone, getting whiplash left and right, or suffering from a headache as a result of an ugly argument, can I whisper something in your ear? Jesus said you will have trouble in this life – and this can include trouble within your closest relationships.

So, if that's unavoidable, then what matters is how you handle that trouble. How you respond when you want to drive your bumper car right into the other person is what makes a difference.

Unlike bumper cars, the Spirit of God living in us allows for a gentle response when our hearts have been hurt and want to hurt back. You might just have to step off that dangerous ride, walk down the street, grab some cotton candy, and invite the Lord back in when your heart is hardened and angry.

When we give ourselves permission to pause, to shut up, and to pray when we're angry, we can discern if God is giving us words to speak or the wisdom to not speak. If you turn your ears to that before you fight back, I promise you'll cause less damage AND your relationships will be sweeter in the long run (cotton candy kind of sweeter).

GET IT OUT

What are you angry or frustrated about? Who have you been butting heads with, and how has this affected the relationship? What about with God? How have you responded when God doesn't act the way you think He ought to and it's difficult to understand Him? BE HONEST!

_____

_____

_____

_____

_____

_____

_____

_____

_____

_____

TRUTH SAYS…

John 16:33 is the truth that we will face trouble in this life. Jesus didn't say we MIGHT have trials but that we WILL have trials. We will bump into each other. We will face conflict and sometimes it will give us a horrible headache. But there is a hopeful message here too: conflict won't overtake those who believe, because Christ has overcome the worst that the world could throw at us.

1 Corinthians 13:4-5 reminds us that love is patient. Consider how patient the Lord is with us when we don't understand. We ought to let that be our motivation for practicing patience toward those we don't understand, including God's ways and timing.

2 Timothy 2:23-24 reminds us not to give ourselves over to foolish arguments. Don't step into the bumper car ride just for the heck of it.

James 1:19-20 is a powerful piece of truth that encourages us to listen more and speak less. If we listen closely, God will give us words to speak and wisdom to not speak at the appropriate time.

James 4:6-10 encourages us to draw near and humble ourselves before God when our human nature wants to build walls around our hearts. Pride is a form of self-protection, but this passage reminds us that we have no need to protect ourselves when we have a God who protects, preserves, and lifts us from the enemy.

THE BIG IDEA: A HARD HEART BRINGS HURT, BUT A HUMBLE HEART BRINGS HEALING

Day 14: seeking or settling?

John 4:31-34
Psalm 81:2
Luke 14:15-24

A few weeks ago, we failed to make reservations at our favorite restaurant for date night. After driving 30 minutes with eager hearts and empty bellies, we nearly sprinted through the doors of the restaurant only to find out there was over an hour wait.

WHAT?! ARE YOU SERIOUS?!

Although we were irritated, we opted to check out the restaurant across the street.

Epic fail. 45 minute wait there, too.

IS IT THE-WHOLE-TOWN-EATS-AT-ONE-TIME-DAY OR SOMETHING? SHEESH!

At this point I was really annoyed and Matt was growing hangry-er by the minute.

I looked across the room and saw another couple close to our age enjoying a wonderful meal. I instantly grew jealous.

WHY CAN'T WE HAVE WHAT THEY HAVE RIGHT NOW?

We put our names in and stormed off more dramatically than necessary. How dare they not know we were coming?

Okay not really, but we were frustrated. We didn't want to wait any longer than we planned on. In fact, we were so hungry that we decided to get dessert first. You know, to keep our blood sugar up. We both ordered large waffle cones and gazed at them lovingly as the little blonde ice cream scooper lady handed them to us. We literally inhaled them in 60 seconds. I even had to wipe drops of ice cream out of Matt's beard.

As we left the ice cream parlor, we began talking about what we were going to order at dinner. We talked about steak and mashed potatoes and warm soup. And then it dawned on us that the ice cream had helped but it didn't quite do the trick. We were still hungry.

When our table was finally ready, we sat down to enjoy a delicious four-course meal. Our bellies were finally full. I even fell asleep on the way home. That's when you know it was good.

So, what's my point?

Sometimes when we feel sick of waiting on something our hearts long for, such as love or companionship, we turn to ice cream cones. In other words, we begin to settle for whatever's available rather than waiting on what's best. It's as if our hearts are so hungry as we wait and wait, as place after place we seek satisfaction from fails, that we settle. Sometimes, it can become far too easy to settle for a man that's not good for us, just because our hearts need that quick little fix.

Isn't it funny, though, how we still feel hungry, or lonely, or unsatisfied?

Something is still missing – it's not quite enough. I know because I've done it. Maybe you're thinking, "Big whoop. She's married."

Well, yes, but that doesn't just turn off lonely. I've felt lonely time after time, both in and out of a relationship. I get antsy when Matt doesn't text back. I question if I'm a burden to him. I wonder if he misses me when we're apart. I spend countless hours shuffling through lies in my head telling me I'm not quite miss-able or noticeable or love-able enough. Just like you do, girlfriend. Whether you're single or madly in love, I'm a firm believer that loneliness has very little to do with a relationship status. But it has everything to do with God calling us to be alone with Him.

So, if you're feeling lonely and tired of waiting, let

me challenge you to look at what you're filling yourself up with. Is it an ice cream cone, or in other words, just a romance that isn't all that good for you? OR is it the real deal?

I'll bet if you wait and seek a little Him, your place at the table will be ready, because you've been invited to His Great Banquet.

So, RSVP and show up.

He will satisfy that grumble in your belly and craving in your heart.

GET IT OUT

Write down everything you've been trying to fill
yourself with that isn't God. Have you been
tempted to or have you chosen to settle for a guy
who doesn't lead and love you well? If you are
currently in a healthy relationship, ask yourself
honestly where you've been drawing your
identity from: the guy or God? Have you been
seeking Him or settling for him?

TRUTH SAYS…

John 4:31-34 is the words of Jesus discussing the food our spirits need to function properly. The food our spirit needs is His presence to fulfill the calling to which we've been called.

Psalm 81:2 is God telling the Psalmist (and us) that if we open our spirit to Him, He will fill us with good things deep in our innermost being

Luke 14:15-24 is the parable of the Great Banquet. Jesus tells this parable to illustrate our attitude toward God. He's invited us to the greatest feast, to dine in the Messianic Kingdom. Our place has been prepared. But when we chase after the appetizers this earth offers, we tend to make excuses not to attend His great feast. This hurts God because He loves us and wants us to taste of His glory.

THE BIG IDEA: SEEK HIM AND SHOW UP

Made in the USA
Lexington, KY
17 August 2017